The Stable Boy

CHRISTIAN SCRIBER

TO EMILY
FROM Timothy J Scriber

authorHOUSE®

CHRISTIAN SCRIBER AT.ATT.NET
CHRISTIAN SCRIBER @ATT.NET

AuthorHouse™
1663 Liberty Drive, Suite 200
Bloomington, IN 47403
www.authorhouse.com
Phone: 1-800-839-8640

First published by AuthorHouse 01/05/2008

ISBN: 978-1-4343-5328-3 (sc)

Library of Congress Control Number: 2007909108

*Printed in the United States of America
Bloomington, Indiana*

This book is printed on acid-free paper.

A Message from the Author

This is a fictional story, but there are scriptural references that are left to the reader to indulge in with his/her own Bible for the clarity of the *fact and truth.*

The message in this book is important!

The story was written in a fashion so as to get the reader's attention as to where the world is standing in perspective to where we will all be going one day. It helps us to understand how we should be living our lives in today's world in order to obtain a place in **God's Kingdom.**

It is a story of faith and trusting in **God's** plan for individual lives as well as for the world.

References

Romans 8:28

And we know that God causes *all things* to work together for the good to those who love God, to those who are called according to *His* purpose.

Romans 8:29

For whom He foreknew, He also predestined *to become conformed* to the image of His Son, that He might be the first-born among many brethren;

Romans 8:30

and whom He predestined, these He also called; and whom He called, these He also justified; and whom He justified, these He also glorified.

Revelation 10:7-10

But in the days of the voice of the seventh angel, when he is about to sound, then the mystery of God is finished, as He preached to His servant the prophets. (8) And the voice which I heard from heaven, I heard again speaking with me and saying, "Go, take the book which is open in the hand of the angel who stands on the sea and the land." (9) And I went to the angel, telling him to give me the little book. And he said to me, "Take it, and eat it; and it will make your stomach bitter, but in your mouth it will be sweet as honey." (10) And I took the little book out of the angel's hand and ate it, and it was

in my mouth sweet
as honey; and when
I had eaten it, my
stomach was made
bitter.

Table of Contents

CHAPTER ONE
Charlie's Introduction

Hi, my name is Charlie. I'm a mouse. I'd like to tell you a story about my life. Actually, it's a story about a boy whom I met who helped me understand what life is all about.

I had heard from other mice that years ago there lived a very nice elderly man who had taken care of the villagers' horses throughout the years, and it was said he was the finest horse groomer that ever lived. It was told that the old man had a beautiful wife and several very mannerly children, and that a fire in their house had taken all their lives except for the youngest son. The story continued that the boy went to live with his grandmother who also lived in the Village and who was ailing. She welcomed his company and help.

As the story was told, the grandmother died very suddenly with many unpaid debts. In order to pay off the debts, the Village bank took her home and farm and put them up for sale. This left the boy alone with no place to live.

No one in the Village could afford to take care of the boy and they felt very sad. All the villagers held a meeting because they wanted to help the boy. It seemed to them that the boy was very apt in taking care of himself since he had always helped his father with the household chores and the stable business.

At this meeting, the villagers agreed that if the boy was willing to live on his family's farmland, they would all work together and build him a small house and Stable. This would enable the boy to make enough money grooming horses to support himself, and give him a purpose for his life. He would also be able to carry on with his father's trade.

Even though the boy's father's trade was a horse groomer, and this was a trade that the boy would grow into, the villagers at this time considered him *"the Stable boy."*

Oh my! What a fine time this turned out to be for the villagers! They all had known the boy's family and had come to love and respect his father for the grand way he cared for their horses. The whole ordeal seemed to give the villagers a good sense of purpose as they worked together helping the boy.

Well, as I was being told this story, the people of the Village had just finished building the little house and Stable. Since my family and I had been living under an old stack of wood out back of where the original house had been before the fire, we were so happy to see the boy living there again. It was always nicer when people lived close to us. It meant more food and better shelter for all of us mice.

I'll never forget the day the boy moved into the new house. Everyone from the Village came out. They brought food, furniture and supplies for the little house and Stable. They had a picnic that lasted all day. My, my, my! The feast of crumbs left behind actually could feed all our mice friends and my family for the winter.

The boy was very busy the first day in his new home. He had decided to water and groom every horse that was pulling a cart or had been ridden by one of the villagers that came to his house that day. As a matter of fact, he was so busy that he did not even notice that my family and I were busy making a new home in the Stable. Oh, WOW! A new front door hole, new hay beds, tons of crumbs from the picnic to store for the winter, everything we needed to make a home. We were as busy as the new owner.

The next day, we slept in all day and we assumed the boy did the same, as we didn't see him the entire day. Early in the evening we heard noises at the big door to the Stable. I told my wife and children to be very quiet, and I would go see what was happening. I hid behind a small box of nails left by one of the villagers who had helped build the Stable. As the big door slowly opened, I saw that it was the boy. He was yawning and still appeared tired from sleeping the whole day. The boy immediately began cleaning the mess he had left from grooming all the villager's horses from the day before.

As I watched him, I could tell why the people cared so much for him and his family, especially his father. The boy, so I was told, was like his father in looks and manner. He seemed tall (to me) and muscular and ruggedly dressed. He appeared to be very easy going and meticulous at his work. His face was very gentle, and he whistled a lot. It made me feel happy.

Suddenly, the boy turned quicker than I had anticipated and he saw me looking at him from behind the box of nails. He was startled, but not scared. To my surprise, he said, "Hi, mouse!" To his greater surprise, I said "Hello!"

He said, "Why, you are quite amazing." I said, thinking he spoke of my good looks, "Why, thank you. I do groom myself well. I also have a small gym in the back of my house where I work out. It keeps me looking fit to where people notice, as you did."

The boy laughed and said, "No, I didn't mean you were quite amazing in how you look. I meant it is quite amazing that you talk." I said, "Well, why are you so amazed? All mice talk." The boy laughed again, and said, "I've never heard mice talk before." I replied, "Well, most often people and animals are chasing us more than stopping to talk with us. We are kind of talked to, but not with. We usually get pretty scared because we are so small. So we run away and hide."

Much to my surprise, the boy very slowly and gently reached his big hand down and put it around my little hand and said, "I'm pleased to meet you. My name is Chris. What is yours?"

I said, "We don't have names. We just know each other and get along pretty good without names. Since we will probably be talking again and I want to tell my family about you, could you give me a name?"

Chris said, "You look like a Charlie to me. Is that okay?" "Sure," I said, thinking to myself that in human, it probably meant *strong and handsome* or something like that. At any rate, it kind of gave my mouseness a little humanness. "Thanks, Chris," I said and we shook hands again.

Chris said 'Good Night' to me and went into the house. He was tired after his long day of working in the Stable. I was so happy that we were friends.

CHAPTER TWO
Chris' Memories

*T*he next morning after Chris had slept
till near sun-up, he jumped to his feet,
stretched and yawned. He then knelt
down next to his bed to talk to God. "Father
God," he started, and then after thinking for a
moment, he said, "I guess now You are my only
Father, and I guess I want to let You know that
I wholeheartedly choose to honor and serve You
as I served my own father. I'm glad my dad and
mom and family are with You. I know they are
safe and happy, but I miss them so much. **God,
please help me to figure things out,** and to

help me do a good job in caring for the villagers' horses as my father did. Well, I better let You get back to the more important stuff You have to do. Will You please bless all the villagers that helped me, and bless my new home? Oh, yeah! Please bless my new friend Charlie and his family, too. Thanks, Dad. AMEN."

As Chris started looking around his new home, he missed seeing the things that surrounded him when he was in his parents' warm, simple, little home. It seemed like everything in it spoke of who they were and what they loved: pictures, flowers in vases, things carved by the children which they gave as gifts to one another for their birthdays or at Christmas, things that mother had knitted or sewn thrown over the end of a couch or chair to warm them in the chilly evenings. It made Chris' heart ache when he thought about his family, as he had been surrounded by so much love and caring and now, it was gone.

As Chris glanced around at the furniture and the boxes of things that some of the villagers had brought him, he suddenly noticed a box that had "VERY IMPORTANT" written on it. Hurriedly, he opened it to find to his delight that someone had sifted through all the burned ruins from the old house and had found pictures of his family. As he lifted them out, there in the bottom of the box was his father's Bible. Chris was so happy and excited because this was not just any old book. This was his father's way of living according to his Heavenly Father. Every word was underlined once, twice, three times— words circled, words and sentences highlighted, names of his children, his wife, his neighbors and friends inserted into the pages surrounded by God's promises and guidance.

As Chris looked through it, he thought to himself, "This isn't just dad's Bible. This was dad's instructions from God and his diary between him and his Heavenly Father."

In that moment, Chris realized that Father God answered his prayers and had given him *both* of his fathers' instructions: his earthly father (human), and his Heavenly Father (spiritual). He knew in his heart that **he would be able to figure things out** and everything would be okay.

Chris spent most of the day going through the half worn-out pages of his father's Bible. By the evening, he thought about Charlie and decided to go to the Stable to visit him for a while.

CHAPTER THREE
Chris Meets Mike

When Chris opened the door to the Stable, he was surprised to find Charlie whistling quite cheerfully and sawing boards with a tiny saw. Charlie wasn't surprised when Chris opened the door this time, as he had hoped Chris would come to visit. After all, it wasn't too often that people and mice got together and talked. So he was quite pleased to see Chris.

Chris leaned over and took Charlie's little hand in his and very gently but tightly shook it and said, "How ya doin', Charlie?" "Just fine, Chris. How are you?" Charlie replied.

"I'm feeling quite a bit better. I found some family pictures in a box, which the villagers brought to me. At the bottom of the box was my father's old Bible. I am so happy to have these, especially the Bible. It kind of settled me in my spirit," Chris answered.

"What are you doing with the saw and boards?" Chris asked. "Just making a food pantry for our house," Charlie replied.

Chris sat down on a little stool and started to chuckle. "What are you laughing about?" Charlie asked. "Oh, it just seems funny to see a mouse with a saw making a food pantry," Chris answered. Charlie laughed, too, and said, "Well, we mice have lives, too, ya know. It's not like we can have the town carpenter come out here and crawl in our hole and build things for us."

Suddenly, Chris put his fingers to his lips and said, "S-H-H-H," to Charlie. "I think I hear footsteps outside the door." There were several knocks on the door. Chris, thinking it was someone from the Village and not too afraid, opened the

Stable door. There standing in the doorway was a very unusual, to say the least, person. It was a man in his younger years with a skin tone and hair that literally glowed from the bright moon that was shining directly behind him.

"Hello, my name is Mike and you're Chris, aren't you?" Chris, a bit sheepishly said, "Yes I am, but who are you and what do you want with me?"

"Well, my dear young man, I have a request of you that I know you are up to. I'm sure after you hear what I have to say, you will consider it to be in your best interest," Mike replied. "Well sir," Chris replied, "since you are a stranger, I'm not sure that you truly know what is in my best interest."

Mike smiled and said, "Chris, through the Master I serve, I have been given knowledge of you and your family which extends quite a distance back into your family history."

"Did you know my father?" Chris asked apprehensively. "Yes, quite well," Mike answered.

"Your father was also a servant of my Master for many years. He served him in body and spirit. There was no finer man in his family bloodline. I thought at one given time that he was the last of his line, but it turns out, as I was informed by my Master, that you, dear Chris, are the last."

Chris interrupted and said, "Sir, without any insult to you, I would certainly wish that you would quickly come to the point as to why you are here."

"Yes, of course," said the stranger. "My Master requires your service as a horse groomer: boarding, feeding and grooming a special horse. However, at this time, I will leave a lot out of what I am to tell you. I will fill in the information in more detail at a later time."

"You see, Chris," Mike said, "I am the one who brought this same horse to your father years back. When I approached him about caring for the horse, he did not have the time, nor did he need the money. His business, as you will remember as a child, was doing very well and the

Village, itself, was prospering from their crops and stores. I told your father that he needed to take twenty-four hours to think this agreement over and to pray and consult God through his Bible in what he should do, as the horse would take a lot of his time and care."

Mike's voice went from telling the story to a command, "Chris, this is the same thing you must do."

Mike then went on with his story saying, "After much prayer, your father agreed *in faith* to take care of the horse. He accepted what his Bible told him, *that God would provide for those who have complete faith in Him.*"

Mike continued, "The Village people, as it was well known, were a *Godly* lot, but they had fallen on hard times due to the on-going drought. A lack of crops and failing businesses had affected the entire Village. It had even affected your father's business and income. Even though the Villagers' horses were not as fine as other horses in the nearby villages, they all felt that your father's skills made their horses look as fine as any man's horse. Your father was getting up in years and it was becoming very difficult for him to care for his family, not to mention, the horse that I had left with him. Your father was a strong man of faith and had always trusted God to take care of his needs. The fire that had started that night was not God's idea, but He did use the circumstances for the best outcome."

"Now, Chris," Mike continued, "I must tell you something and you will have to believe me as to why I know these things. At this time, I cannot tell you how I know, but I will answer all at a later time. I want you to know that when the fire started at your home, it was on the outside. Sparks from the chimney dropped to the dry grass around the house and ignited the grass. Your entire family was sleeping. All died peacefully in their sleep. None of them suffered. Chris, I promise you that I am telling you the truth. You were the only one who escaped because *you* heard the horse kicking out the side of the Stable to escape the fire. As the intense heat and the wall of flames drove you to escape through your bedroom window, you had barely crawled but a few feet away before you passed out. Chris, believe me, there was nothing you could have done even if you had not passed out. The horse, after escaping from the Stable, dragged you by your clothes to safety before it ran away."

Mike continued, "Chris, as I said before, you need to pray to God and read your father's Bible. **You will be able to figure things out and you will know what you should do *before*** you accept the responsibility of the horse. You also should consult the Village people as to what they might do to help you take care of the horse. Then after twenty-four hours, you can give me your answer."

Chris sat very silently after Mike had stopped talking and then after several minutes said, "Mike, I think I want to go to bed now. I am very tired. So will you please excuse me? You are welcome to return tomorrow at the same time, and we will talk more about the horse. Thank you for speaking with me."

Mike said, as he opened the big door to leave, "Good night, and may God bless you. I will see you tomorrow night."

Chris and Charlie looked at each other in wonderment.

They both said "Good night, see you tomorrow." Chris went into the house and went to bed. Charlie crawled into his hole amazed by what he had heard.

Chapter Four
Meeting With The Villagers

When Chris woke up, he lay still for a few moments thinking about his talk with Mike the night before. He thought about his family and about his need to get to the Village early so he could talk to the villagers about the whole ordeal with the horse. The rest of his thoughts, he knew, needed to be on his knees at his bedside.

"Father God," he started. "If I'm not interrupting anything right now, could I please talk to You about some things? I'm sure You already know what I'm referring to, but **I need**

to figure it out for myself. I had thought about things a while last night before I went to sleep and had tossed it around in my mind that, maybe, Mike was an angel sent by You; and even possibly he might be Jesus. I know he was no mere man because he looked very different and had great knowledge of so many things. Dear Father God, I do believe in my heart that You want me to freely choose for myself what You are asking of me and that it is something You desire for my life. As I go to the Village today, please direct my footsteps to the villagers whom You know will help me. I *step out in faith* in doing this, as I only want to do what will honor You. Please bless my day. Thanks, Dad. Amen."

As quickly as he could, he put together a bag of homemade muffins that some of the village women had made for him and a jar of fresh-squeezed lemon juice in water to take with him for his day's visit in the Village. He didn't want to burden anyone with feeding him, or to take up too much time at any one house.

As he walked to the Village, he saw Matthew Isaiah, the owner of the town livery stable, walking from his house on his way to work. He quickly ran and skipped a few steps to catch up with him. "Hi, Mr. Isaiah," Chris said.

"Hi there, Chris," said Mr. Isaiah. "It's good to see you out and about. How's that new place of yours coming along?" he asked.

Chris replied, "Oh, fine, sir. I was most blessed to find a box of pictures of my family and my father's Bible in a box that someone had left at my house. It was kind of the person to sort through the burned remains of the house to find them. It meant a lot to me."

"Oh, that was Tim Scriber," said Mr. Isaiah. "His whole family line has always been into genealogy and he's always trying to help people get to know their family roots. Tim's kind of the Village 'know-it-all.' He talks a lot, but he means well. You'd probably enjoy talking with him. Your father seemed to enjoy his company. Tim told me he had spent many a grand evening at your family's home talking with your father and enjoying your mother's fine apple pie."

"Putting that aside, Chris, is there anything that my family and I can do for you, anything at all?" asked Mr. Isaiah.

"Well, no sir, not exactly for me," Chris replied. "But there is something I need to speak to you about. It may seem a bit strange, but it is true. A stranger, who called himself, Mike, came to my house yesterday evening. Actually, he came to my Stable where I was spending time talking to my friend, Charlie, who is a mouse."

"Whoa there, Chris!" Mr. Isaiah exclaimed. "You were talking to a mouse, you say? Well, Chris, I think my family and others from the Village had better start inviting you to our homes for companionship. It sounds like you're getting a bit lonesome – talking with a mouse, huh."

Chris continued, "This Mike has asked me to take on a great task that he is assured I am up to. He told me to take twenty-four hours to pray about it, which I have; and to seek counsel of the

Village people, which I am doing now. Still, I am not sure that I am up to the task he has set for me."

"Does this have anything to do with a horse, a particularly special horse?" asked Mr. Isaiah.

"Why, yes! How did you know?" asked Chris. Chris was amazed that Mr. Isaiah had knowledge of the horse.

"Chris," Mr. Isaiah said, "this is a very, very important matter of which we are about to speak. I must ask you if you are agreeable to meeting with several of the villagers at the same time to discuss it in its entirety. Chris, go to Mark Zechariah's down the road, one house past the general store. That is where we will have our meeting. He and his wife should still be there as it is still early in the day. Tell them that I have gone to fetch Luke Jeremiah and John Jacobson to bring them to the meeting. We will be there directly. Hold your conversation about this matter until we have all arrived."

Chris ran down the road until he came to Mr. Zechariah's house. As he stood knocking on the door, he thought to himself, "I hope the Zechariah's do not feel an intrusion with all the company they are about to have so early in the day."

Mrs. Zechariah opened the door and seemed very happy to see Chris. "Come in, Chris," she said excitedly. "It is so good to see you. Mark and I are presently enjoying a glass of milk and a fresh piece of apple pie. Will you join us? I do believe that you will enjoy the apple pie, as I went to great lengths to pry your mother's recipe from her."

As Chris came into the house, Mr. Zechariah came across the room to greet him. Outstretching his hand and gathering Chris's hand in a firm grip, he said, "Young man, you are the mirror image of your father, both in manner and looks. It is so good to see you. Are you well, I hope?"

"Oh yes, sir," Chris replied. "However, I feel as though I need to be doing something soon, so as to stay fit both in mind and body."

They sat for just a while when Mr. Isaiah and the rest with him stood at the screen door, looking through it and bidding good morning to Mark and his wife.

"Come in. Come in," Mrs. Zechariah called out to them. "Join us for pie and milk." Everyone came in, husbands and wives, at the call of pie and milk. Times being hard as they were, not everyone was fixing pies and bakeries on a very regular basis.

Into an hour of eating and exchanging greetings, Matthew Isaiah spoke out in a rather loud and deep voice, "Well, everyone, I'm sure you all would like to know the reason I asked for this meeting. We, being the Village elders and council, I felt that we should represent the entire Village in the matter of which I am about to speak."

"From what Chris has informed me of this morning," Mr. Isaiah continued, "the horse is back! Well, he's not exactly back, but Mike has approached Chris in a quest to return the horse to Chris' care. Chris has also told me that he has no income or money of any sort to support the care of the horse. We all know that Chris' father cared for this same horse for several years during the prosperous times of our Village."

"Even though we had to take our horses from Chris' father's care for various reasons, he didn't need any financial help caring for *this horse* because he also raised crops of grain and was financially fit. Chris is not. He is asking for our support, both in feed and finance. Mike has not said anything to him about paying for his services. I know that all of us are pretty much in the same situation when it comes to our savings, as we all had taken what we had to build Chris his house and Stable." Upon hearing this, Chris felt an overwhelming sense of love for the villagers, as they had sacrificed so much for him.

Mr. Isaiah proceeded, "Mike did tell Chris that he would give him a day's time to make up his mind. He is to return to Chris' house this evening. He told Chris to seek God's council as well as ours."

"Now first," Mr. Isaiah continued. "Let me redirect this conversation back to you, Chris. All of us know about the horse and about Mike bringing the horse to your father one evening many years ago. Very slowly, but with much secrecy, your father told us a few things about the horse."

"There is something we want you to know and that is how much we trusted and respected your father," explained Mr. Isaiah. "As a matter of fact, we overwhelmingly voted your father to lead us, the entire Village, in a weekly prayer and bible study. We all joked about his last name being Christian, and said, 'Who better to lead us, if not a Christian?'"

"Your father took this as being an honor from all of us, as it was intended to be. I suppose there's not one individual in the Village that your father had not personally prayed with at one time or another. Over the years, your father led us in *trusting God in faith* for everything. Even more, he taught us about the blood sacrifice of Jesus Christ who suffered, died and rose again for our redemption. Many of us even thought that your father could be the coming Messiah. There is no one whom we have ever known that led a cleaner, more loving, godly life than your father."

After several hours of talking mostly on various subjects other than the matter at hand, they did talk about how the entire Village was of one mind in serving God in whatever manner they were called to help.

They also talked about how through the years each family--one after another—had been *tested in faith and character* and how after being tested, each family came to a greater understanding and love of God the Father and a deeper knowledge of who they were IN CHRIST JESUS, and who CHRIST WAS IN THEM!!

At the meeting at Mark Zechariah's house, each person, husband next to wife, knelt in silent prayer seeking guidance from God on the matter of the horse. After a while, they all began to stand one-by-one, and then took a seat. After all were seated, Mr. Isaiah spoke out again, this time softly and directly, "I think we need a written vote on this matter."

"Give me a moment," said Mrs. Zechariah. "I'll get some paper and pencils." She quickly passed them out and all the couples, without writing anything down, stood up and began clapping in Chris' direction. This was the answer Chris longed for in his heart. Without saying a word, they were agreeing to help take care of the horse financially and with its feed. Chris was overwhelmed.

He thanked everyone. "Now," he thought, "I am ready to give my answer to Mike."

He was so happy and thankful that he skipped and whistled all the way home.

CHAPTER FIVE
Mike Returns With The Horse

When Chris got home from his visiting with the town's people that afternoon, he worked around the yard for a while planting new flower starts sent from the town's folk today. He cleaned up around the yard and broke ground to start a small garden.

Thinking over how good he felt about the way the friends of his family had received him today, it was like they were his family now. After working for about an hour, Chris decided to get cleaned up, have a little lunch, and take part of a muffin out to the Stable for Charlie and his family.

Chris was whistling, as usual, as he came up to the Stable and Charlie heard him. So he ran to the big door to wait for him to come in. When Chris unbolted the door handle from the outside, Charlie grabbed hold of the door as high as he could reach to help pull the door open. When Chris threw the big door open, Charlie went for a little ride, holding on for dear life. Chris saw him holding onto the door as he came in and said, "Hi, Charlie, you tryin' to close the door shut on me?" Then he laughed.

Charlie was glad to see Chris in a good mood, as the last time he had seen him, he didn't look too high in spirit. Mike had told him about his family passing away in the house fire, and Charlie felt really bad for the way Chris seemed to have taken the news.

"Charlie," Chris said, "I have some good news to share with you. I talked to the town's people, and they all agreed to help me with the task that Mike has asked me to take on. I do so hope after your hearing the conversation with Mike last evening and the news that I have just shared with you, that you and your family will find it well to have the Stable and your house shared with another occupant."

Charlie, without a moment's hesitation said, "Chris, this all belongs to you. If you choose it, my family and I will move out to another place."

Chris interrupted him and said, "Charlie, we're all family and I not only want you here, but I'm sure I will need your help and counsel."

Charlie had never gotten even close to a human, but he came over and put his little arms around Chris' ankle and hugged it as hard as he could. "Thanks, Chris," Charlie said as a little tear rolled down his cheek.

It was just about dusk in the evening now, and Chris was getting pretty anxious about Mike's return. Chris thought to himself, "What if he changed his mind? Maybe he found someone better suited to the task." Chris said a soft prayer, "Dear Father God, please let everything be okay for the safety of Mike and the horse. I know I acted like I didn't want this responsibility at first; but once everyone was okay with it, I knew that it must be **Your** will, too. I don't know just everything that this endeavor will require, but I do know that **You** will help me through everything. Thanks, Dad. Amen."

Chris heard a rustling around the ground outside, not exactly like footsteps, but he was sure it was Mike. One loud knock on the door and then the door latch lifted and the door swung open. "You in there, lad?" asked a loud voice that Chris recognized as Mike's.

"Yes, sir, I surely am," replied Chris.

Suddenly, there stood Mike in the doorway with the moonlight behind him giving him that strange glow. This time a very unusual horse stood next to him. The horse's outline and its large size were giving off the same glow as Mike's.

Chris stood very wide-eyed and quite stunned. Charlie ran into his hole and hid, thinking it would be better to listen than to be seen.

Mike reassuring Chris said, "Fear not. For what you see as the moon glowing on me and the horse is called *The Spirit of God's Anointing* over us. I would like to introduce you to this magnificent animal. Chris, this is HIS MAJESTY, the HIS, meaning my Master. The horse is simply called, MAJESTY. You will soon come to know that this horse is anything but simple."

Mike asked, "Well, Chris, have you taken the past twenty-four hours and prayed and sought the counsel of the Village?" Chris answered, "Yes, sir, I have."

"Then may I ask if you have made a decision about boarding and caring for HIS MAJESTY?" asked Mike.

"My answer is said from my heart, as well as with my mind," responded Chris. "My entire life I have always tried to please God, my Father.

I feel now that this is somehow very special between God and me. This horse seems like a gift to me, or maybe it will be my gift to God. My answer is YES-YES-YES! I thank you for choosing me for this great honor."

"Your bloodline, Chris, is the reason for my bringing this horse to you," continued Mike. "Your bloodline, Chris, is your family descendants from generation to generation. Look in your father's Bible and it will tell you about the bloodline of many people in the Bible especially that of the Messiah, Jesus Christ. It will help you to understand a little better about the significance of a family's bloodline."

"Chris," Mike said, "I will tell you more about HIS MAJESTY's bloodline at a later time."

Mike continued, "I will explain some things to you now that will make you understand all of this a little more clearly. Chris I am an angel. My full name is *Michael, the Archangel.* My Master is God, Himself, and I have served

Him in many ways through the ages. This task He has given me now is one of the finest things He has ever had me do. I do so enjoy being around you humans on earth. All of the angels have knowledge of who you all are *in Christ*. We can't wait to show you where we come from. The appointed time is coming soon."

Chris took care of MAJESTY, bedding him down in the Stable and feeding him as Mike instructed. Mike left for the night and said he would return tomorrow and give him more information regarding MAJESTY.

Chris said, "Good Night" to Charlie and went into the house. He was anxious to find out what bloodline meant. He took his father's Bible off the table that was near his bed and started to read about the bloodline of Jesus Christ. As he was reading the story, he started falling asleep and then thought about MAJESTY, "Wow!! I can hardly wait to hear about MAJESTY's bloodline."

Chapter Six
Majesty's Bloodline

Mike had explained to Chris that he was Michael the Archangel and that God had sent him to earth to bring the horse named HIS MAJESTY to Chris.

Mike began to tell Chris the story about MAJESTY's bloodline, "It was a couple thousand years ago in Judea in the City of David called Bethlehem. It all began with a little donkey and the birth of a very special baby, Jesus the Christ. The little donkey and several other animals gathered in the manger that first night and witnessed the birth of the Messiah that the prophets had spoken of for many years. No person or animal would be the same now that the Messiah was here."

"Joseph, Jesus' earthly father, and Mary, his mother," Mike continued, "did not spend much time in Bethlehem after His birth. They stayed only to sign the census, as there were people who wanted to harm them. They needed to go to another region in order to be safe."

"The only reason they went to Bethlehem for the census was that Joseph was of the family bloodline of the House of David. He had to return to Bethlehem with his family in order to be counted," Mike explained.

"One night an angel appeared to Joseph in a dream," Mike continued, "and told him to take Mary and the baby, Jesus, and flee to Egypt. They were to stay there until it was safe. Joseph quickly woke Mary and Jesus. He put them on their donkey and they went to the land of Egypt. The angel appeared to Joseph again and told him it was safe to leave Egypt and they were to return to Nazareth."

"Once in Nazareth, Joseph decided to breed the donkey with a gentler breed of mule. It was a little larger animal than the donkey and would be much better for family travels. It would also be worth more money in the event they chose to sell it. In those days men in the stable business bred animals such as horses and mules in order to get a better breed of horse." Mike stopped talking for a moment.

He said to Chris, "I do not choose to minimize nor take away any details of Jesus' life; but for now, I must tell you the story about the horse. Since you will be taking care of MAJESTY, it is important for you to have this information."

Mike continued with his story, "As a result of the donkey being bred to the mule, a new breed of mule was born. Just as the first donkey had been at the birth of Jesus in Bethlehem, the first mule in the new breed encountered Jesus as a grown man when he was starting His ministry on earth."

Mike continued, "Jesus and His closest followers were preparing to make an entrance into the city for the believers to receive Him as their leader. Jesus told His followers to go to a certain house and ask the man for his mule so He could use it to ride into town. The men obeyed. They went to the man's house and found that the man's mule had recently given birth to a fine colt, but the man said that the mother mule had difficulty giving birth to the colt. The mother mule had been bred to a larger mule and the colt was larger than normal. The men took both the mother mule and the colt to Jesus. The mother mule became sicker as they arrived at Jesus' location. Jesus looked at the mother mule and said to the men, *The mother will not survive, as she is too ill. Stay with her and cover her with blankets and keep her comfortable until the end. She will be at peace now.*"

Mike went on with the story. He said, "Jesus rode the young colt into the city while the people waved to Him and threw palm leaves on the road. While Jesus was riding the colt, the colt felt like something quite unnatural was happening to it. It felt like it was somehow, changing inside. As the colt walked through the streets, it felt the weight of the MESSIAH on his back, *the very flesh and blood of Jesus the Christ.* As the colt moved along, he had an overwhelming feeling of both pain and delight. His mind was seemingly thinking thoughts as a human might do. To the colt's understanding he realized that he was carrying someone who was going to change his and everyone else's lives from then on. As Jesus rode on the colt, Jesus' anointing was going into the colt, *Spirit and Body. The colt was to have no other master or purpose in his life than to serve as HIS MAJESTY."*

Mike stopped talking once more and after a moment, said to Chris, "I believe you humans call this experience being *BORN AGAIN.*"

"This colt was to be the start of a whole new *anointed* bloodline in complete service to God Himself. Each horse born, thereafter, throughout the generations was named "HIS MAJESTY," because each was *anointed* to God's service," Mike explained.

As Mike concluded the story about MAJESTY's bloodline, he left Chris with instructions as to MAJESTY's care. He told Chris that he must never ride the horse or allow anyone else to ride him. HIS MAJESTY must never be used for any task or work. Any waste left from the horse's care was to be left in buckets for someone to remove from the Stable at night. Promptly at sunset, Mike himself would come every evening to take the horse out for its exercise and he would return within an hour. "Chris you are to handle your affairs of the house as well as your evening meal at this time," Mike instructed.

Mike saw Charlie standing just outside of his hole listening very earnestly. Mike bent down and carefully picked up the little mouse and said, "Hello, Charlie. How are you and your family doing?"

"Pr-pr-pretty good, your honor, sir," responded Charlie.

Mike laughed, "Well, Charlie, you don't have to call me sir or your honor. We angels are very like humans in some ways. Mainly we are all servants, just as you are. Coming from where the Master lives does give us a *"little"* edge on things."

Charlie had a lot of questions for Mike, but all he could do was stutter. He knew about angels from stories from other mice over the years. He had even thought he had seen one several times, but this one was holding Charlie in his hand and talking to him. Charlie thought to himself, "Boy, I wish some of the other mice could see me now."

Mike gave Charlie a gentle little rub on his head with one finger and said, "Charlie, the task I have given to Chris is extremely important. I must ask that you help Chris in any way that you can. Everything you see or hear must be kept secret between the three of us."

Charlie, not knowing what to do, held up one hand and said, "I swear." Mike laughed and said, "Well, maybe you better not do that." Then they all laughed.

Mike stayed a few minutes longer and then left. Chris spent some time brushing MAJESTY and preparing his bedding of hay. As Chris stood on a stool to reach the horse's head and shoulders, he noticed that bones at the very top of the horse's front shoulders pushed hard on the skin. He thought it was solid muscle because of the horse's excellent physical condition. MAJESTY looked like he could out run the very wind.

Chris finished his chores and said, "Good night," to Charlie. Then he left the Stable to go to his room to pray and sleep.

CHAPTER SEVEN
Mike's Trick

When Chris woke up the next morning, he felt renewed in body and spirit, because he now had a sense of purpose for his life that was beyond his expectations. As he lay in bed, he thought about his father and how he must have felt having to keep MAJESTY a secret from everyone, even his family. Chris thought of how it would have been if his father were still alive and how they could have shared the secret together. It would have made them closer as father and son. Then he thought of Charlie and how lucky he was to have him as his friend and remembered that he was not alone in knowing the secret of MAJESTY.

Chris quite eagerly rolled out of bed and in a single movement landed next to his bed on his knees, very anxiously wanting to talk to his Heavenly Father. "My dear Heavenly Father," Chris began, "I am surely glad and honored that You have brought me to this very wonderful place in my life. I know that it was through my father's obedience to You that all these blessings have come to me."

"I do, so very much," Chris continued, "want to let You know *I am, because You are.* Take my things that I accomplish today, add the guidance of Your Holy Spirit, and the assistance of Your angels to help mold myself into the character of Jesus Christ that I may bless You this day. Thank You, Dad, for everything. In Christ image, I pray. Amen."

Chris spent much of the day planting his little garden and pulling more weeds. Whistling and freely talking to God, it almost seemed to

Chris that there would be no need to go to heaven if everything stayed this nice right here. Then Chris thought a bit more about heaven and said, "Except I want to see my family. It says in Dad's Bible that when I go to heaven, I'll live with God forever, and I don't want to miss that."

Several times during the day, Chris went to the Stable to tend to the horse. Mike had brought with him a large bag of feed and a large bag of hay for bedding the horse. As the day went by, Chris knew that the supplies he had would last the rest of the day. So he would go to the Village the next day to get more feed and hay from the villagers. "Oh, my!" Chris thought. "If only the villagers knew who the horse was." But that was not for him to tell.

As the day closed out to dusk, Chris had waited eagerly to see Mike again. Mike knew so much about everything and was a much friendlier angel than Chris thought angels would be. As he started out to the Stable, he suddenly found Mike walking beside him. "WOW! That was cool," said Chris. "How did you do that? One minute you weren't here and then the next, you were walking beside me."

"Well, we angels have our moments," Mike replied. As they walked along, Mike put his arm, or Chris thought it was his arm, around Chris' shoulder. To Chris' absolute wonderment, Mike had these beautiful, white, soft, feathered wings. "How's that for a good trick?" Mike asked Chris.

"Will I ever have those, too?" Chris asked. Mike replied, "There are things that you do not need to know just yet. Some things need to be revealed at a certain time. I think you call that, *a need-to-know* thing. Actually, Chris, you don't really need wings down here. You have horses to ride." They both laughed, Chris knowing that he had just heard some angel humor.

As Mike and Chris entered the Stable, Charlie was right there to meet them. This time, he was standing back away from the big door. He wasn't going for that ride again. Both Chris and Mike shook his little hand and bid him a smiling, "Hello."

Mike was the last to shake Charlie's hand and he still had his wings out. Charlie looked at them and said as quickly as Chris had, "Will I ever have those?"

"Why does everyone want to fly?" Mike asked.

"Oh, I don't want everyone to have them, just me. I think they are really cool. I would like to see things from a higher place than I've been used to," replied Charlie.

"Charlie," Chris asked, "where have you been all day? I've been to the Stable several times today and didn't see you at all."

"Well," said Charlie, "I am much like Tim Scriber in the Village. I'm sort of a *know-it-all* among all the mice. Not nosey, mind you, just curious. I spent much of the day visiting other mice all around the Village, mostly in stables where they live. Wherever I went, my friends were very surprised to hear that I had so much to say about nothing.

As I have been sworn to secrecy of the goings on at my own home Stable, I had to stick to small talk. I guess that might be a mouse joke, right?" Mike smiled rather than laugh at Charlie's seriousness.

CHAPTER EIGHT
Charlie's Bloodline

"**M**ike," Charlie asked, "would it be alright for me to tell Chris of my bloodline, and do you know it yourself?"

"Yes," Mike replied. "It is alright to tell Chris now; and yes I do know of your bloodline."

Charlie stood on top of the little sitting stool, so as to give him a higher eye level to all as he began to speak. "Chris, I want to tell you of my bloodline because of the bloodline of MAJESTY."

Charlie continued, "My bloodline started some two thousand years ago in the town of Bethlehem, in the same Stable where the baby was born. There was a relative of mine named Chucky. Even though we mice don't have names, he gave himself one."

"Anyway," continued Charlie, "Chucky spent that night in the Stable. Fearful of being seen and possibly chased off for being too close to the baby, Chucky hid under the blankets lying in the hay."

"When the mother gave birth, the father reached over and picked up the blanket to cover the new baby. Chucky held on tight to the blanket. He found himself lying on top of the little baby's chest. As Chucky lay there, concealed by the blanket, he could feel the warm breath from the baby's mouth. As Chucky listened to the people talking to each other, he heard that the father of the child was named, Joseph, and the mother's name was Mary. They talked several times to the shepherds who were there tending to the Stable animals.

Chucky listened fearfully for hours to the parents talking about their baby and who He was. Chucky thought to himself, "If this baby was, indeed, who they say, then humans would surely become better people because of Him. Maybe, even humans and animals would get along better."

Suddenly, someone picked up the baby. It was the mother and she was preparing to feed Him. As the blanket was pulled back away from the baby's face, Chucky was totally exposed. "Oh no, I'm dead now," Chucky thought.

"Hello, little mouse." It was a very pleasant and soft voice coming from the mother. "Don't be afraid, no one will harm you. I know that you are a good little mouse because you made no attempt to harm my child or to run away." The beautiful lady stroked Chucky's head softly and said, "Would you like to be introduced to Jesus, the KING OF KINGS and LORD OF LORDS?"

"Yes, please," Chucky replied.

Mary, the Mother of Jesus, took Chucky in the palm of her hand and said, "Jesus, I would like to introduce You to this little mouse. What is your name little mouse?" "Well, we don't really have names, but I call myself, Chucky," he replied.

"Well Chucky, meet Jesus. I am Mary and this is my husband, Joseph," said Mary. "The Stable boy tending the animals is named Chris." This was to be the first of two encounters Chucky would have with Jesus.

Thirty-three years had gone by and Chucky moved several times over the years. This time he hid in a bag of clothing and was taken on a caravan to Jerusalem. As he was hiding in the bag that was stacked on the camel's back, he could hear the voices of the caravan travelers talking about the coming events that were to take place in Jerusalem, the town to which they were going. It seemed that someone was trying to overthrow the king. He couldn't hear the complete story. "Well," he thought, "this has little to do with me."

Chucky's main concern at the time was to move to a bigger city in hopes of finding a nice girl mouse to be his wife. The last town he had lived in was mostly inhabited by rats. By any mouse's standards, RATS were UGLY, especially the females. Mice stayed clear of all rats.

When the caravan finally arrived in Jerusalem, Chucky crawled out of the bag of clothes and made his way to the first house with a stable. As he crawled into the hay in back of the stable, he heard horses going by outside and people yelling loudly. It sounded like there were a lot of angry people going by. They were yelling, "Crucify him! Crucify him!" Chucky waited until the angry crowd passed by, for fear that if they saw him, they might try to harm him. As Chucky ran along the streets as close to the walls of the buildings as he could, he heard several people yell from the crowd, "Jesus of Nazareth, King of the Jews!"

Then Chucky thought to himself, "Oh, this must be that person who is trying to take over the king's throne." Certainly that was not a very good thing to try. It seems to have made everyone pretty mad. Why do they keep hitting him and spitting on him? Why do they want him to carry that big tree thing on his back? Even if he's a bad man, why not just make him go to jail for whatever he did.

As the crowd left town though the gates in the wall, they soon arrived at a large hill. As Chucky climbed up the hill, he was having a very difficult time because he knew he had to stay off the road or he might be seen. By the time Chucky reached the top of the hill, most of the crowd was on the way down.

Chucky hid behind a big rock until no one else passed by for a long time. Then he ran out on the road and hurried the rest of the way to a flat clearing at the very top.

As he looked ahead, he could see that there were three tree-like things standing up straight out of the ground and there were men, somehow, hanging on them.

As Chucky got closer, he could see that
the men were not moving. When he looked at
the men, he saw that they were all bruised, badly
beaten and were no longer breathing. Chucky
noticed that several women were sobbing softly
beneath the man in the center.

Very quietly, Chucky moved closer to the
crying women. As he looked into the face of the
woman in the center, she looked down at him
and even though she was barely able to speak, she
reached out her hand and stroked Chucky on his
head and said, "Hello, Chucky."

It took but a second and Chucky knew
who she was. "Aren't you, Mary, Jesus' mother
that I met at His birth?" Chucky asked.

"Yes, I am," Mary said.

Chucky knew he shouldn't, but he asked,
"What did He do and why did they do this to
Him?"

Mary took a moment, breathed deeply
and said, "Well it's like this, Chucky, Jesus is the
Son of God who lives in heaven. He came to this

earth to be punished and to be put to death for the sin of all mankind."

Mary continued, "Men were not perfect enough *nor animals that were sacrificed* for the original sin that man is born with. The *sin of disobedience* that Adam and Eve committed while they lived in Paradise was never totally forgiven between man and God. Therefore, God sent His only Son into this world, birthed inside of me by the *Holy Spirit of God,* to come and pay the price that man could not pay. A blood sacrifice was the only way. *Greater love has no man than to give his life for another."*

Mary looked up very sadly at the cross her son was on and said, "LOVE had to die so that LOVE could be born again."

By now, Chucky was sobbing uncontrollably and had his little head lying on the top of Mary's foot. "Mrs. God," Chucky said, "if I want to be *born again,* can I?"

Mary, smiling softly, bent down and picked Chucky up in her hand and brought him close to her face and said to him, "Dear, sweet Chucky, my Son died for all and that includes even animals. But I need to tell you something more clearly. To start, I am not Mrs. God. I am Mary, a normal human being, who by the power of the Holy Spirit, conceived in me, Jesus, the human being. He was both God and man, but I am neither God's mother nor his wife."

"I was born without original sin," continued Mary, "so that Jesus would be born in a holy bloodline. Even I must believe in Him for my salvation."

"Now concerning your being *born again,*" Mary explained, "I will tell you this. You, Chucky, have never committed sin against God, so being born again is not a necessary thing for any kind of animal. God does give favor to animals as well as humans as they have lived, be it good or bad. The rats that you have seen in your lifetime are a good example of this, because they live in rebellion to both man and animals. You Chucky, have come from a fine bloodline of mice, and your first meeting with my Son at His birth has given you great favor with Jesus' Father in Heaven."

Mary continued, "If you recall those thirty-three years ago as you held onto the blanket that my dear husband threw over Jesus as he lay in the *feeding trough,* you were lying on little baby Jesus' chest under the blanket. As you may also recall, Jesus breathed on you; and as you breathed in His very breath, you received the *Holy Spirit* into you."

As Mary, very gently, sat Chucky back on the ground, she said, "Chucky, you are now able to serve God to your utmost as you are transformed by His Holy Spirit. You will be able to enter heaven someday because you now have God's LOVE in you."

Charlie said, "As the years went by, Chucky and all the mice he talked to became increasing interested in the affairs of human Christian believers. Many a mouse would devote their entire lives to living around these humans and helping them in any way possible. The Christians did not know this was happening. As time passed through the centuries, many a mouse found his reward in heaven."

"As the years passed into at least two thousand," Charlie continued, "it came to pass that a certain mouse and his family took a ride in a hay wagon that they were accidentally thrown into by a stable boy. They were lifted into the air and thrown into the wagon of hay that was on its way to market in a village called Antioch. The stable boy was lifting hay from the stable where the family lived and was filling the wagon with hay when it happened. To say the least, the mouse family was utterly surprised and frightened to have been removed from their home in that manner."

"As they arrived in the Village, they were thrown with a stack of hay into the Stable of a young boy who had just recently moved into the house. This is where we live today," Charlie said.

CHAPTER NINE
Six Bags

"Well, Chris," said Charlie, "I guess this is the time when you and I first met. As you will remember, you were cleaning the Stable and you saw me hiding behind a small box of nails. After saying hello to me, I answered and you were surprised that I could talk. Since then, you and I have been talking to each other every day."

"As I have related the story of my bloodline to you Chris, I'd like to ask Mike a question. Mike, is what I have told Chris all of the truth?"

Mike replied, "Pretty much word-for-word."

Chris asked Mike, "After hearing about the bloodline of MAJESTY and Charlie, is there a chance that I could be related to the shepherd boy named Chris, who was at Jesus' birth that night in Bethlehem?"

Mike pondered the question and then replied, "Chris, there is a man named Tim Scriber in the Village to whom you need to ask these questions. He had a fall from his horse several years ago and has remained blind since that time. You need to seek him out. He also needs you at this present time. I can tell you no more of this, but don't delay your visit."

"Now, Chris," Mike went on, "I have given you verbal, as well as written instructions on the care of MAJESTY. Before I leave, I have something to present to you."

Chris and Charlie followed Mike outside, as he had brought a large, gold-covered box with him and had not taken it into the Stable. He opened the box and began removing bags of something from it, six in all. He sat the bags on the ground and told Chris that there was a bag for him and one for each of the villagers: Tim, Luke, John, Mark, and Matthew. Then he untied the string on one of the bags, opened it and handed it to Chris and said, "This is for you to help out with your finances."

As Chris took the bag from Mike, it was so heavy he nearly dropped it. As he opened it and looked inside, he said in disbelief, "Is this what I think it is?"

"Yes, Chris," said Mike. "It is a bag of gold nuggets."

"Where did you ever come across such riches?" Chris asked.

Mike threw his head back and laughed heartily. "Chris, where I come from, gold is lying around the streets."

Mike then told Chris, "Each person that receives one of these bags of gold will be those that are directly involved in the care of the horse.

They will receive the gold since they *stepped out in faith* to help you with your endeavor, even though they had little or no resources to do so. My Master has chosen to reward them for their deeds. You may only tell them, for now, that the gold came from the horse's Master through me. They will also find it a wise suggestion, from you, that they should begin to buy seed for the coming year, as they will be blessed with many good seasons of planting from now on."

"It takes *faith* to please my Master," Mike continued. "He rewards greatly. I must bid you farewell for now, as I have much to do in a very short time. Be blessed Chris, and you also, Charlie."

"Good-by, Mike. Thank you," both Charlie and Chris spoke at the same time. Mike then disappeared into the night.

CHAPTER TEN
Tim Meets Mike

*Q*s the twilight of the sun came over the hills that surrounded the Village, the morning dew caused a cloudy haze that filled the air around Chris' house. He had been in a deep sleep and woke with a sudden jolt. He felt as though he was still asleep. He quickly looked out the window and saw the foggy air outside. "Had all this been a dream?" he asked himself. As he crossed the room to wash his face at the kitchen sink, there sitting on the table were six bags. He opened one and there it was, GOLD!!! It had not been a dream. He washed his face, got himself a drink of water and then excitedly in a very loud voice said, "WOW!"

"Father, God," Chris began. Without kneeling, but rather standing with his eyes closed and his hands raised, "You are certainly an awesome God. I know that *through Christ,* that makes me an awesome person. May I be worthy of Your calling on my life. Please bless my day, and everyone that will be in it. To Your glory, I totally submit myself to You. Thanks, DAD, my God. Amen."

As Chris quickly packed a bag of lunch to take with him as he went to the Village, he was thinking of a few things that he needed to do today. First, as Mike had told him, he must hasten to visit Tim Scriber. He quickly picked up a bag of gold nuggets to give to Tim, as Mike had directed. He also put half a dozen apples in a bag for Mr. Scriber. The apples were from Chris' mother's own tree that was in the yard behind the house. Chris put all these things in a small pull cart, making it easier to carry the bag of gold.

Boy, will Mr. Scriber be surprised—apples from Mrs. Christian's own tree!

As Chris started walking away from the house, pulling the cart behind him, he glanced over near the Stable and saw Charlie digging very earnestly in the dirt next to the Stable. "What ya doin' there, Charlie?" Chris asked.

"Putting in a garden," replied Charlie.

"I wouldn't plant any watermelons if I were you," replied Chris. Both laughed and waved to one another.

As Chris arrived at Mr. Scriber's house, he looked through the screen door into the house and spoke loudly, "Good morning, Mr. Scriber. It's Chris Christian. May I come in?"

"Yes, of course, Chris," answered Mr. Scriber. "I am truly glad that you have come to visit."

"Well, sir," said Chris, "I do have some pleasant business with you today. I'm sure that you will agree."

"What might that be, young man?" replied Mr. Scriber.

As Chris shared his entire story with Mr. Scriber, a loud knock at the door startled both of them. Mr. Scriber asked Chris to see who was at the door. "Since I lost my sight after falling off my horse, I can only tell who is at the door if they speak out to me. Be the person friendly, Chris, ask them in," said Mr. Scriber.

As Chris went to the screen door, he was pleased to see that it was Mike. "Hello," Chris said. "Please come in." Chris and Mike went into the room where Mr. Scriber was sitting. Chris said, "Mr. Scriber, I would like to introduce you to Mike. He's the angel I told you about."

Mr. Scriber was still pondering in his mind all that Chris had told him. Mike moved closer to Tim, then he lifted his arms straight out to his side and immediately his large, white, flowing wings appeared.

Mike said, "Tim, come to me and use your hands to feel all around me. You will be able to see, through the touch of your hands, who I am." As Tim touched Mike's wings, he began to smile and then to laugh and then to cry. "I always knew that angels were real, but it was always a *matter of faith,* and *believing but not seeing.* Now that I can finally believe and see, *I am a blind man."*

"All things work together for good for those who are called of the Lord and obey," Mike said. "I must leave you now. So you can conclude your business with Chris. I highly recommend that you pray together before Chris leaves. Goodbye," Mike said. "You be blessed, both of you, in the Name of the Father."

As Mike closed the door, Mr. Scriber took Chris' hands in his and said, "Chris, let's pray now. Dear precious Lord, we humbly come before You to ask for Your guidance in the matters of the affairs that Your servant, Michael, had brought to us. Help us to always see Your will with our hearts rather than with our eyes."

Chris closed his eyes and then began to pray. He said, "Dear Father God, I ask that this servant of yours be blessed with clear vision and that his eyes be opened so that he may give you glory." As Chris was praying he put one of his hands over Mr. Scriber's face and the other hand was raised toward heaven. Chris continued his prayer, saying, "We serve you willingly, Father. Thank you in the name of Jesus, Your Son. Amen."

As Chris opened his eyes, he saw Mr. Scriber putting out his hands for Chris to lead him. Chris took his hands and led him to where two rocking chairs sat next to the fireplace. Both began to sit down at the same time, hitting their heads together quite hard. Mr. Scriber fell back into the wooden rocker very hard, breaking off both the rocking chair's legs. He fell very hard on the edge of the stone fireplace, and hit his head with a loud thud.

As Chris helped Mr. Scriber to his feet, he turned in Chris' direction. "Oh, my dear, God!! Chris, I can see!! I can see!!" exclaimed Mr. Scriber.

With blood slightly trickling down the side of his head, Mr. Scriber grabbed Chris' hand

and both began dancing all over the room. After much joyful laughing and a goodly amount of praising and thanking God, Mr. Scriber sat down and said, "Boy, Chris, I didn't see that coming." They both laughed.

Chris then picked up the bag of gold and handed it to Mr. Scriber. As he opened it, he couldn't believe his eyes. He was overwhelmed by everything that had taken place that day. He said to Chris, "Now I can start back into my business of genealogy studies. This is the tracing of family bloodlines to as far back as I can find documentation on the family descendants."

"I was unable to read or write for several years because of my blindness," continued Mr. Scriber. "Even though I have been a poor man, God has always supplied my needs through my good neighbors in this Village. Now I have new hope and purpose to live for. Is there anything at all that I may bless you with, Chris?"

"Well, sir, there is one thing that I might ask of you. Could you possibly trace my family bloodline? As you know, my family passed away in a fire and I have yet to have a proper stone for their cemetery plots. I was thinking of putting a family crest on their marker stones."

"Chris, I think that this will be my first endeavor as I start up my business again," replied Mr. Scriber. "Thank you, Chris for everything. It was a pleasure to meet with you and also to meet Mike. It has been quite an experience today. I praise God for healing my eyes so that I may see. Chris, I will be in touch with you once I find information on your family descendants."

Chris left Mr. Scriber's and walked home. As he walked, he thought about the miracle that had just taken place. "God is wonderful. He meets all our needs," said Chris.

CHAPTER ELEVEN
Antioch Gold Rush

fter spending the entire day at Tim Scriber's, Chris arrived back at his house just around dusk. He had hoped that he would get to the Stable while Mike was still around. He felt that he needed to discuss some things with him about the last four bags of gold.

As he came close to his house, he saw that the Stable door was open and he heard Mike and Charlie talking. He put his pull cart next to the Stable. He started whistling loudly as he walked into the Stable so they would know who was coming. It wasn't likely that he would scare

Mike, but sometimes Charlie would get a little startled when he heard someone coming. "Hi, Mike. Hi, Charlie. How's everything here?" Chris asked.

"Okay," Mike replied. "Did everything go well today with Tim and you?" Mike was grinning as he spoke. Chris was sure that Mike already knew about Tim's eyesight being restored.

"Yes," Chris said. "Everything went just as if it was all meant to happen the way it did."

"Yes, you're right, Chris," Mike said. "But sometimes, God hides things in a manner to where you can judge it either way. Keeps folks from thinking they know how to push God's buttons for the things they want. Tim's a good man and he's been in a lot of God's plans over the years, but it was considered that Tim needed a few years rest so he could draw closer to the Father. I gotta give God that," Mike said. "He sure knows what He's doin'. Sometimes we angels try to figure out what He's up to, but we usually guess wrong."

While Chris started cleaning and grooming MAJESTY, he asked Mike about how he should present the gold to the villagers without letting them know too much.

"Well, Chris," replied Mike. "I was talking to God about that very thing this morning. His thought was that we should grind the gold nuggets to dust and plant it in the old mine that collapsed back in their great grandparent's day. All the streams that lead to each house are directly connected to the mountain that the old mine was in. God decided that He would do another one of those *'judge-it-any-way-you-want'* kind of things. This way, they will have to work a little for it. Kinda have their own little gold rush. He knows quite well that the Village already knows that *every blessing comes from His hand*.

The news about Tim Scriber's sight returning was noted by the Villagers to be the *Hand of God*.

Little-by-little, the town's people started noticing gold sparkles in their stream water. It was soon found out that it was indeed, **PURE GOLD!!!**

Each household fixed their watering pipes to a filtering system that filtered them a nice amount of gold dust each month. There was plenty of gold to live on and plenty to help others, too. It was decided in a town meeting that the gold must be kept a secret so that people from other villages didn't over-run the Village population or over civilize it. Both of these things would lead to greed and crime.

The villagers continued with their farm life and their businesses. They were always sending money to other town's people or anyone who might need help as they heard of the need. They never told anyone about the gold.

CHAPTER TWELVE
The Antioch Church

Q few years had gone by, and it seemed as though the Village was *growing more in stature* than in size. Everyone felt that God had lifted many of their burdens, had blessed them and had answered their prayers in getting them through the years of drought.

Tim Scriber bought a horse and buggy and was doing a lot of traveling from town-to-town, doing research on individual's family descendants, as he was still in the genealogy business. He charged a nominal fee for his services. His clients were mostly people in the

Village or from surrounding towns. There were a lot of people interested in their family history. Tim would put together a booklet with all the information he found on a person's family with a cover that had a very nice picture of their family crest.

Chris had hired Tim to follow his family bloodline quite a long time ago. Chris was waiting to receive information from Tim regarding his family.

It seemed to most everyone who hired Tim to research their family descendants that he could trace anyone right back to Noah or even further in some cases. Anyone who knew Tim also knew that his entire house was full of files and records of family histories. Some people laughed about it and said that Tim was probably in charge of *God's Book of Life.*

From time-to-time, Tim would come back to the Village to take care of local business and he would usually pay Chris a visit. At one particular visit, he had discussed with Chris as to whether

Chris knew of anyone who might have use for his large, empty barn. In past years, Tim's father had farmed hay and used it for winter storage. It just seemed a shame to leave it empty according to Tim.

Chris was quick to reply to the offer. It seemed that the Village people wanted Chris to lead them in some type of bible study or even Sunday services. No one had a large enough house for any more than six or eight people to come at one time. Most people's houses were fit for their families with no extra rooms. A few people, as the town was now prospering, were building on an extra bedroom or so. Hardly anyone considered building extra rooms that were not for sleeping in. Sometimes a grandparent would pass away and the family might build an extra bedroom for the remaining grandparent to stay in if they visited or moved in.

Chris had tried to visit with different families at different days of the week so as to have a bible study that would accommodate more people in a week's time. As it had been going so far, quite a few families just had their own bible studies in their home with their own family. If Chris was able to use Tim's barn, they could all assemble together at one time. At least on Sunday, when people need to stop their busy week, they could spend some time in neighborly communion and *worship to God.* Chris had even thought that if ever the town had a Sunday meeting place, they might call it ANTIOCH. This was the same name of the Village, but Chris knew from the Bible that ANTIOCH was the first Christian church.

Tim liked the idea, and told Chris to use the barn with his blessing. Tim told Chris, "Ya know, God likes to take empty things and fill them with Himself."

The Village people were so excited about the whole idea of a church for the town that most of them wanted to have their first meeting the very next day, and this was only Monday. Plenty of the people got together right away and helped

Chris clean the old barn inside and out. Some people even planted some flowers and little trees around the outside.

John Jacobson, who owned the General Store, furnished and installed some real nice windows and a very attractive wooden door for the front entrance. John was actually the one who had first talked to Chris about leading the bible study. Very soon, John and his wife were the greeters at the door as people would come into the church.

Matthew, Mark, Luke and John, after a period of time, became the church elders. It seemed as though everyone in the Village had a special place of service in the church.

Chapter Thirteen
Chris' Bloodline

*L*ate one afternoon, Chris was taking some quiet time going through some bible verses that he wanted to share with the Village folks at the next church meeting when he heard noises at the front window. He looked out and could see Charlie on the ground throwing small pebbles at the window. Since his knock on the door was not too loud, Charlie did that sometimes to get Chris' attention. As Chris opened the front door, he saw Charlie about as frightened as he had ever seen him. Charlie was trying to talk, but could only stutter. He kept pointing toward the Stable and moving in that direction. Chris knew it was something serious. So he picked up his father's old, long-barrel gun that had been sifted out of the ashes of the house fire years ago. His father had kept the gun in the house to chase off an occasional bear or stray dog. Who knows if the gun would even fire? Chris cleaned it and kept it loaded, but he had never actually fired it.

Chris quickly picked up a log branch in his other hand. As he and Charlie moved toward the open door of the Stable, Chris could only imagine something very vicious and wild would be inside of the Stable.

Charlie was able to mutter a few understandable words between stuttering: "huge, hairy, strange feet, fangs for teeth." Chris moved quietly along the side of the Stable, readied the gun in one hand and the log in the other. He jumped as far as he could and landed right in the middle of the open doorway. Waving the log and yelling at the top of his voice so as to scare and surprise whatever was in the Stable.

To his surprise, Mike was standing in the Stable petting MAJESTY. Standing beside him was a baby lamb.

Chris yelled for Charlie to come in, but he wouldn't. So Chris went out and carried him into the Stable.

"What's going on, Chris?" Mike asked. He was quite surprised at the entrance they had just made.

"Well, Mike," said Chris. "It seems that Charlie had seen a monster in the Stable and ran for his life. He told me that the monster had fangs for teeth and some other horrible things."

Charlie stood there with his head hung down. Looking a little sheepish himself, he said, "Well, it was dark and I couldn't see real good."

Mike and Chris got a good laugh over the whole thing and so did Charlie.

Mike picked up the little lamb and handed it to Chris. "The Master wants you to have this little lamb, Chris. He said that there are many lessons for you to learn about sheep and flocks and shepherds."

"He also told me," Mike continued, "that it would be a favorable time to tell you a little more about your family bloodline. As you have been hearing from Tim Scriber, he has been very earnestly pursuing your heritage."

"You, Chris," Mike explained, "have come down through these years in a very, very clean and holy bloodline. The Master has always been very pleased with the generations of Christians and Shepherds. It seems that there have always been just about as many preachers in your family heritage as any line on earth. Moreover, the Master has bid me to inform you that your bloodline, indeed, does go back to Bethlehem: back to the Stable, back to Jesus birth, and back to a shepherd boy named Chris and a *baby lamb* named Jesus."

CHAPTER FOURTEEN

Chris' Birthday

I t was a cool evening and Chris was sitting in front of the fireplace in the rocking chair. The logs were crackling and popping and flames were dancing all around in the fireplace. It was one of Chris' favorite times of the day. His family had always gathered around the fireplace after one of his mother's delicious meals. His father would always read from the family Bible and nearly always told a story that he'd heard from someone, which was usually Tim Scriber. Tim had many adventures in his life.

As Chris reflected on the past years since his family's passing away in the house fire, he thought of how the village people had built him a house and a Stable. And how he had met Charlie, his little mouse friend. How he had met Mike and MAJESTY and how he now raised sheep for enough years that he now had a very large flock. He also thought of the little baby lamb that Mike had brought to him and how over the years he learned more and more of how to lead his church flock. Surely, these were the lessons that Father God knew Chris would learn from the baby lamb.

Jesus was the first lamb in the flock. Chris, the shepherd boy back then, was the first shepherd to tell everyone about Jesus. After these many years, it was all down to the shepherd and the flock. What a wonderful feeling, Chris thought, to know that you have always been in God's plan – ALL OF US.

As Chris sat rocking and thinking over his few years on earth, he realized that it was only

two days until his birthday. Tomorrow night was
Christmas Eve and the next day was Christmas,
HIS birthday. He had always loved it over the
years that he was born on Christmas day, because
he would receive presents for Christmas and his
birthday. It always seemed like every year he and
Jesus shared something, always there for each
others birthday. It was even more significant
now since he knew of his family bloodline.

Every year the villagers held a party for
Chris on Christmas Eve at the church. It was
actually the day before his birthday. After church
service on Christmas, everyone stayed home all
day with their families.

This year Chris was going to be thirty-three
years old. Knowing Jesus lived for thirty-three
years made Chris wonder how long he himself
might be around.

This year the villagers had told Chris that
they had special gifts for him. They told him
that they would come over to the house early
Christmas Eve to present gifts to him. They also

said that God had directed them to do so and that he would understand the importance at a later time.

The following day was Christmas Eve and Chris was very curious as to what the villagers had planned for him that evening. As Chris went through the day, his thoughts were about the village people—knowing now what a wonderful feeling it was for his father to live here and lead the flock that God had given him. Each family that Chris now helped out and ministered to had become his family as if they were the same bloodline. Chris thought to himself, "This has got to be how Jesus feels."

After Chris had gone about his daily routine of duties around the Stable and the house, he rested for a while next to the fireplace, sipping a cup of hot chocolate. He had fallen asleep for a part of the afternoon and was awakened by the sound of horses, wagons and people singing. As he stood to his feet, he could hear that it was the villagers. All were singing Christmas carols and were quite happy and cheerful. As Chris opened the front door to greet them, they all started singing "Happy Birthday."

One-by-one, they presented Chris with their gifts. Some were large and heavy and some were very small. All were cheerfully wrapped and decorated with ribbons and bows. Everyone told Chris that he couldn't open his gifts until his birthday.

It was somewhat chilly out that evening and the villagers sang a few more Christmas carols and then headed back to their homes. All bidding Chris good fortune and that they would see him in the morning for Christmas church.

That next morning Chris arrived a little early at the church so he could spend a little extra time in prayer and private communion with Father God. As the village people arrived, it warmed Chris' heart to be with so many people that he had grown to love so dearly.

The church filled up quickly. As Chris stood before them, he began to speak to them about Jesus' birth as a *New Beginning* and then His death as *an End to Something* —SIN itself. And then he spoke of Jesus' resurrection as a *New Beginning* for men to be *Born Again,* Holy Spirit filled and able to live in the likeness of Jesus in their lives.

"Now," Chris said, "we are coming, as I have so often taught you, to the end of an age. And we must be preparing for another new beginning. As Christ has lived, so must we live. And where Christ has gone, so must we go. Not to an end, but to a beginning."

As the church service ended and all joined together in worship to God in one accord, Chris was glad to realize that the final alter call this year was not responded to by anyone, as in prior years. From time-to-time a stranger would come to a church service and receive Christ as his Savior before leaving. Tonight, it was just all family.

After church, everyone shook Chris' hand and wished him a Merry Christmas and Happy Birthday. After leaving church and heading home himself, he thanked God for everything he had. Not things, but possessions of love in his heart that he had gained through the years.

As Chris approached his house, he saw Mike sitting on his porch whittling on a stick and whistling cheerfully. "Good evening, Chris," Mike said. "And might I wish you a Happy Birthday?"

"Why thank you, Mike," Chris replied. "Can you stay for a hot chocolate?"

"I'd like that," said Mike. "Ya got any marshmallows?"

"Sure do," replied Chris. "Come on in."

As they sat and talked for a while, Mike pointed to all the gifts. "Ya mind if I stay while you open your gifts? There's a thing or two I want to tell you as you open them."

"Sure," said Chris. "I'm pretty curious of their contents anyhow. So why don't I start now." As Chris began to open all the gifts, he was surprised to see that all the gifts were fine horse apparel. Chris had no horse of his own and was never to ride MAJESTY. He wondered as to why all the villagers had given him horse apparel. Chris looked all of the gifts over very carefully and said to Mike, "I think that the metal in all of these gifts are made of some really special metal."

"That's all pure silver," Mike said. "Since the Village has prospered over the years, each person has made their individual item out of the finest leathers, cloths, and metals that they could find. They had all, at one time or another, given over to the idea that you could be the returning MESSIAH HIMSELF."

"Today is Christmas," Mike said. "It's Jesus' birthday. It's also your birthday, Chris, and you are thirty-three today. To help you to understand, let's take all of these gifts to the Stable."

After Mike and Chris had taken everything to the Stable, Mike brought MAJESTY out of his stall and stood him in the middle of the room. As Mike began putting the different apparel on

MAJESTY, it was obvious that each item fit perfectly: the blanket, the saddle, the mouth bit, the stirrups, and the reins. Each thing that was put on MAJESTY seemed to increase his beauty and splendor.

Chris stood in awe as Mike finished combing out MAJESTY's long, flowing mane and tail. He felt humbled and honored to have been given the opportunity to care for such a beautiful horse.

Suddenly, Chris heard music outside, thinking it to be the villagers. The music was of a sound that Chris had never heard before. Mike looked at Chris and said, "Some of my friends are here."

As if the wind had blown it, the big Stable door opened wide. There were angels everywhere, blowing trumpets and singing. All the angels had beautiful white wings and were flying as if they were birds of the air.

Then, there in the midst of all, stood a MAN glowing as if he were a star from the skies.

All bowed down, including Mike. The MAN spoke, "I'm here for my horse."

Mike looked at Chris and said, "He's here for HIS MAJESTY."

As the MAN mounted MAJESTY, He looked through shining, pearl-like, blue eyes and said to Chris, "Do you know who I am?"

Chris bowed his head and dropped to his knees and said, "MY LORD AND MY GOD!!"

CHAPTER FIFTEEN
An End To Something

As if all time and motion in the entire world had stopped, the MAN seated on the horse said, "I AM THE CHRIST, SON OF THE LIVING GOD."

At that very moment every angel began to sing and many angels with trumpets began to blow them. Then Michael, his wings raised toward the One on the horse said in a voice that shook the entire earth, "AT HIS NAME, EVERY KNEE SHALL BOW, AND EVERY TONGUE CONFESS THAT JESUS CHRIST IS LORD."

Jesus then spoke to Chris, "Well done, oh good and faithful servant." Jesus bent down from His horse and extended His arm out to Chris. He took Chris by his arm and lifted him in one swinging motion and sat him behind Himself.

Chris felt a heavy vibrating coming all through MAJESTY's back. He heard a loud fluttering sound in the air directly in front of Jesus. As Chris looked around Jesus, he saw large, mighty wings extending from the shoulders of MAJESTY. They were extended from the high areas of MAJESTY's shoulders that Chris used to brush over and always thought it to be large bones or muscle. As the beautiful, white feathered wings began to unfold completely, the air all around MAJESTY began to whirl like the wind of a storm or even a tornado. As if by MAJESTY's will, rather than his effort, he began to rise up into the air.

Suddenly, Chris heard a loud noise like the crack of a bolt of thunder and lightning. MAJESTY, Jesus, and Chris were in some other place. It was like the wooden, hilly area that Chris had grown up in, but everything seemed different. The colors were brighter, the grass was a deep, soft green and the air smelled of perfumed flowers.

MAJESTY had taken them to a place where there stood a beautiful mansion-like house. Jesus turned in His saddle and took Chris by his upper arm again and swung him from MAJESTY's back to the ground.

CHAPTER SIXTEEN
A New Beginning

esus dismounted from MAJESTY and walked over to Chris. Jesus looked at Chris and then at the house and said, "Chris, this is yours. You have served Me well and this is your reward. Everything that was left over from your life's service to Me has been used to build this house. Every seed (spiritual or earthly), every twig or leaf, every ash from fire, and even all the left-over things from the caring of MAJESTY in your Stable has been brought by angels to here on a daily basis."

"People from your past," Jesus continued, "whom you helped and who have passed on over the years and people from your past bloodline have worked and built this house for you. There were even those that when you saw their hurts, you prayed for them. You were never able to help them yourself. They also helped to build the house."

Jesus turned to Michael and nodded to him. Michael lifted a trumpet and blew it loudly. Jesus turned to Chris, "Whenever you hear the trumpet being sounded, you must come to its call. It means that the Master is present."

At that moment, Chris noticed that Michael was blowing the trumpet in the direction of a house close by that was similar to his own. The big wooden doors with the golden hinges and handles began to open. Quite unexpectedly to Chris, an angel appeared on either side of the entrance and blew smaller trumpets than Michael had blown. Chris stood in disbelief as he rubbed his eyes to see if he was really seeing what he thought. It was his family. His father, mother and all of his sisters and brothers were standing in the doorway.

Jesus nudged Chris with His arm and said, "Go visit for a while. We'll talk more later."

Chris' visit with his family seemed to be for hours and hours or days and days. There was no sense of time here, no days or nights or places where you had to be. It was eternal. You could go anywhere whenever you wanted to and stay as long as you liked.

Finally after a very long time of talking and laughter with his family which he had missed so badly, Chris bid them farewell so he could go to his own house and look it over.

As Chris approached his front door entrance, Mike came from no where and began walking with Chris. "Hi, Mike," Chris said. "Can I call you Mike here in this place?"

"Yes, Chris," Mike replied. "That will be just fine when we are alone. If others, human or angelic are present, you must respect my authority here and refer to me as Michael. No bowing or hand shaking in those circumstances. Most who have come here have received a new name. Some have received the new name according to their deeds, some according to their bloodline. You, Chris, will remain Chris Christian because on earth and among those here in heaven, you have lived an *above reproach* life. You are worthy of the name that you have. All will refer to you as Chris the Christian."

"Is there anything that you would like to know, Chris?" continued Mike. "Not all answers to everything you ever wondered about will come to you at once, so as not to overwhelm you. There's plenty of time to begin understanding why everything went on as it did in your lifetime. Man's ways are not God's ways, be it in heaven or on earth. God's focus on you right here and right now is: *'Well done oh good and faithful servant. Enter in!'* The Father has much use for you here, Chris, as he did on earth."

"Well, Mike," Chris started. "What about all of my friends? What will they all have to go through? What about Charlie and his family?"

"These are things," Mike responded to Chris' question, "that everyone wonders about as they are transformed into a new life away from everything and everybody that they once knew. To help you to understand, I will let you know some of Jesus' plans. He is going to *rapture* His church out from the earth in the next ever-so-short moments in time. They will be kept from harm as the world begins to destroy itself as the human race. In only a short moment of time here where you are, you will find that the houses surrounding yours will soon be filled with the faithful from your Village. Even their horses, mostly half-breeds of some sort, will be raptured and transformed with them. All the horses will become white as the snow and each will live in their own stable next to their earthly master's house.

"When Jesus is ready to return to earth to finish the battle of men," Mike continued,

"He will have all the angels in heaven with Him and also all the men and their white horses to overcome the evil of the earth that satan has governed over. After this battle, satan will be put away for one thousand years and Jesus will rule the earth. In heaven's timetable, a day is as a thousand. So don't worry about Jesus being gone so long. It will seem only a short time."

As Chris and Mike stood talking, an angel appeared close to them and began to blow a long trumpet. Chris knew what this meant. Jesus had told him that when you hear the trumpet sounding, the Master is present. Both Mike and Chris bowed down and fell to their knees.

There in their midst was Jesus sitting on MAJESTY. "Arise," He said. "Come near to me. I wish to bless you, Chris."

Chris, not knowing what Jesus meant, moved closer to the side of MAJESTY. Looking up at Jesus, Chris said, "My Lord, what is it that You could give me that I don't already have? I am here with You now and forever and I wish for nothing more."

Jesus smiled, pleasured at Chris' pure heart. "My son," He said, "I am about to go into battle with the horse that you have so obediently cared for, even as if it were your own. You have, without any question at all, given to Me all the gifts that the villagers had given to you on your birthday. Chris, what you hold onto is never yours, but what you freely give will surely return. When My battles on earth are finished, MAJESTY will be brought to you as My gift back to you. You are, Chris, a *good and faithful servant.*"

As Chris stood silently and so filled with joy that he thought he might burst, Jesus reached into a large pouch hanging on the side of MAJESTY's saddle and gently lifted out Charlie and his little family. He handed them down to Chris and said, "When I arrived to get you, Charlie was just too scared to leave him there alone. One of the angels built Charlie a little house just like yours, but mouse size, next to your stable."

"Well," Jesus said, "I have things to tend to. It's good to have you here with me, Chris, or should I say *Stable Boy?*"

As He disappeared, He said loudly,

"I'LL BE BACK ! ! !"

LaVergne, TN USA
21 January 2011
213305LV00001B/2/P